TELL ME

DAD

YOUR BEST

STORY

Published by Midsummer Bloom Books

First Edition: May 2025
Printed in the United States of America

Contents

Your Story Starts Here

Remember those moments, Dad? Maybe it was in the garage while fixing something, or during those weekend errands when you'd casually mention your first job, your old neighborhood, or some wild adventure from your younger days. Could've been during a long drive, or while watching a game, or even during those quiet evenings when everyone else had gone to bed. Whenever these stories emerged, we always wanted to hear more.

That's what this book is all about. Because behind being "Dad" – the guy who taught us everything from tying shoelaces to life lessons, the one who worked hard to keep our world turning – there's this whole other life you've lived that we only know in fragments. Not just the chapters where we starred in the story, but the real stuff – like what it felt like growing up in your time, the friends who shaped your journey, or what actually went through your mind when you realized you were going to be a father.

Each page here is just the beginning. A gentle prompt to remember the kid you once were, the teenager with big dreams, the young man figuring out his path when nothing was certain. These aren't just your memories – they're the roots of our family tree.

Take your time with these pages. Maybe stories will come to mind during your daily routine, or in those quiet moments when you have time to reflect. There's no rush, no pressure – just space for your memories to unfold.

Here's the thing, Dad – when you share your stories, even the complicated ones with their ups and downs, you're giving us something priceless. They help us understand not just you, but pieces of ourselves too.

So find your comfortable spot, wherever that may be. Maybe grab that snack you think nobody knows about, settle in, and let the memories flow.

Your stories matter, Dad. And we've been waiting to hear them all.

How to Use This Book

This is your story - there's no timeline to follow, no rules to obey. Choose any question that sparks a memory and begin writing. Skip around, come back later, or linger on the moments that matter most to you.

Remember, these questions are just doorways to your memories. Your answers might lead you down unexpected paths, and that's perfectly fine. This book isn't about perfect writing - it's about capturing your unique journey in your own voice.

Beyond the shoulders that carry us high,

Past the hands that taught us to fly,

Behind the laughter and lessons you share,

Lies a journey of a boy who dared to care.

Before you became our guiding light,

You were chasing dreams, taking flight.

So tell us, Dad, of days long ago,

Of paths you chose and seeds you sowed.

1

Wild Child

Dad, tell us about the little boy you once were! We want to hear about your childhood adventures, the games you played, and the mischief you got into before you became our dad.

Childhood Home

Every home holds countless memories within its walls. What was special about the first place you lived? Think about the sights, sounds, and feelings that made your childhood house a home.

1. What's the most vivid memory that comes rushing back when you think about your first home?

2. Tell me about your favorite spot in that house - what made it so special to you?

3. If you could walk through your childhood neighborhood one more time, what sights, sounds, and smells would you notice?

Family Portrait

Each family member creates a unique part of our early life story. Who were the important people who shaped your childhood? Consider the personalities, traditions, and relationships that formed your first understanding of family.

1. What morning routines from your childhood home stand out in your memory?

2. Who was the storyteller, the peacemaker, the mischief-maker in your family?

3. How did your parents show their love in their own unique ways?

Little Explorer

Kids see the world as a place filled with wonder and possibility. Where did your curiosity lead you as a child? Reflect on the places you explored and the discoveries that sparked your imagination.

1. What mysterious places captured your imagination as a young explorer?

2. Tell me about your greatest childhood discovery - what made it feel so magical?

3. Who were your partners in adventure, and what made them perfect for the role?

Best Friends

Early friendships help shape who we become. Who were your closest companions growing up? Think about the special bonds, shared experiences, and lessons learned through these important relationships.

1. How did you meet your first best friend, and what drew you together?

2. What wild adventures or silly schemes did you cook up together?

3. Did you and your friends have any secret codes, rules, or special traditions?

School Days

Classrooms and playgrounds were the backdrop for many childhood experiences. What moments from your school days stand out in your memory? Consider the teachers, lessons, and experiences that influenced your early education.

1. What moment from your first day of school is forever etched in your memory?

2. Which teacher saw something special in you, and how did they show it?

3. Tell me about a classroom experience that changed how you saw the world.

Trouble Maker

Childhood pranks and mistakes often teach valuable life lessons. What adventures led to unexpected consequences? Recall the times when your curiosity or daring spirit may have landed you in a bit of trouble.

1. What was your most legendary childhood mischief that still makes you grin?

2. How did you face the music when your clever plan went sideways?

3. Was there a prank you pulled that taught you a big lesson about right and wrong?

Weekend Fun

Special times outside of routine school days create lasting family memories. How did you spend your weekends as a child? Think about family traditions, special outings, or simple pleasures that made these days meaningful.

1. What weekend tradition from your childhood would you love to relive just once more?

2. How did your family make even simple weekend activities feel special?

3. Did you ever have secret weekend adventures your parents didn't know about?

Sports & Games

Games and sports teach important life skills beyond just having fun. What activities captured your interest growing up? Reflect on the physical challenges, teamwork, and competitive spirit that shaped your recreational experiences.

1. What was your signature move in your favorite childhood game or sport?

2. Did a victory or defeat teach you an important lesson?

3. Which playground game made you feel like a superhero, and why?

Hero Stories

Everyone looks up to someone during their formative years. Who inspired you as a child? Think about the people—real or fictional— who captured your imagination and shaped your early dreams and values.

1.Who was your first real-life hero, and what made them extraordinary in your eyes?

2. What childhood dream captured your imagination, and why?

3. Was there a heroic act you saw as a child that left a lasting impression on you?

Childhood Challenges

Difficult moments help shape who we become. What obstacles did you face growing up? Reflect on the struggles that tested you and the ways you found strength during those early years.

1. What childhood challenge tested your courage in unexpected ways?

2. Which childhood fear did you overcome, and how did you do it?

3. Who helped you through your toughest childhood moments, and how?

Simple Joys

The small joys of childhood often create our most lasting memories. What everyday pleasures brought you happiness as a kid? Consider the toys, activities, or special treats that made ordinary days magical.

1.What cherished possession meant the world to you, and why was it so special?

2. Which childhood book or story shaped your imagination the most?

3. Tell me about a toy that became more than just a toy to you.

2

Teenage Tales

What was life like when you were our age, Dad? We're curious about your friends, your challenges, and all those stories from your teenage years that shaped who you became.

Growing Pains

The journey from child to teenager brings both excitement and uncertainty. How did you navigate those transformative years? Think about the moments when you began to discover your changing identity.

1.When did you first start feeling like you weren't a kid anymore?

2. How did you handle the transition into your teenage years?

3. What was your most embarrassing moment that you can laugh about now?

High School

School becomes a different world during the teenage years. What was your high school life like? Recall the classes, routines, and experiences that shaped your educational journey.

1. How did you adjust to the changes in high school?

2. How did you manage your time and stay organized with all your classes?

3. Which teachers left the strongest impression on you?

Friend Circles

The people we connect with as teenagers often influence who we become. Who were your important friends during these years? Consider the relationships that provided belonging, laughter, and support.

1. What activities brought you closer to your friend group?

2. When did you meet your closest teenage friends?

3. Which hangout spots became your regular meeting places?

Crush Stories

Early crushes and relationships teach us about ourselves and others. What were your experiences with teenage romance? Think back to those first flutters of attraction and the lessons learned.

1. What made you decide to ask someone out for the first time?

2. How did you handle your first dating experiences?

3. What do you remember about your first real date?

Team Spirit

Clubs, sports, and extracurriculars provide important outlets during teenage years. What activities captured your passion? Reflect on the teams, groups, or hobbies that gave you purpose and belonging.

1. What motivated you to join specific teams or clubs?

2. How did you balance activities with schoolwork?

3. Which competitions stand out in your memory?

Big Dreams

The teenage years are filled with thoughts about what lies ahead. What dreams and goals did you have for your future? Consider the careers, accomplishments, or lifestyles you imagined for yourself during those years.

1. How did you start planning for life after graduation?

2. Was there a dream or ambition you kept to yourself as a teenager?

3. Which adults helped shape your future plans?

Party Scene

Weekend nights held electric promise - each party, hangout, and adventure writing its chapter in our teenage legend. These were the moments when time stood still and anything seemed possible.

1. What activities filled your weekend social calendar?

2. How did you convince your parents to extend curfew?

3. Which social events became legendary among friends?

Summary Freedom

Summer vacations were blank pages waiting to be filled with adventure. Each sunrise promised freedom, each sunset held a story. These were the days when time felt infinite.

1. What responsibilities came with your first summer job?

2. How did you spend your earnings from summer work?

3. Which summer experiences taught valuable lessons?

Life Lessons

Between the laughter and tears, triumphs and mistakes, teenage years forge wisdom in the fires of experience. Each misstep and victory carved lessons into our hearts.

1. What mistakes taught you the most important lessons?

2. How did you handle your first major setbacks?

3. When did you start making more independent decisions?

3

Finding Your Way

How did you figure out your place in the world, Dad? We'd love to hear about your first experiences of freedom and how you navigated those exciting early adult years.

Moving Out

Taking that first step away from the family home marks a significant life transition. What was it like when you first lived on your own? Think about the challenges and surprising moments of this newfound independence.

1. What preparations did you make before moving out on your own?

2. How did you handle those first weeks of complete independence?

3. What important things did you forget to bring when you first moved out?

Money Matters

Managing money becomes a crucial skill when starting independent life. How did you navigate your early financial experiences? Consider your first attempts at budgeting, saving, and making financial decisions.

1. How did you learn to manage your monthly expenses?

2. When did you make your first significant purchase?

3. What budgeting strategies worked best for you in those early years?

Bachelor Pad

A first apartment or home represents both freedom and responsibility. What was your early living situation like? Reflect on the space you created, the challenges of maintaining your own place, and the people who shared it with you.

1. What unexpected challenges came with managing your own place?

2. How did you handle conflicts with roommates or neighbors?

3. What house rules turned out to be the most important?

Solo Explorer

Exploring the world on your own terms offers unique discoveries. Where did your solo adventures take you? Think about the places you visited, the challenges you overcame, and what you learned when traveling independently.

1. What inspired you to take your first independent journey?

2. How did you prepare for your first solo travel experience?

3. What travel mishaps became funny or memorable stories later?

Building Friendships

New environments offer opportunities to connect with different people. How did you create your adult social circle? Think about the meaningful relationships you formed and how they enhanced your independent life.

1. How did you maintain connections with old friends while making new ones?

2. When did you find your core group of friends?

3. Which social activities helped you build lasting friendships?

Life Skills

Living independently means developing practical abilities to navigate daily life. What new skills did you need to learn? Consider the task and knowledge that came with adult independence.

1. What basic adult skills took the longest to master?

2. How did you learn to handle household maintenance issues?

3. Which life skills proved most valuable later on?

Road Stories

Every road holds a story, every journey a lesson. With keys in hand and freedom in the tank, the open road becomes a teacher of independence and adventure.

1. What memorable experiences came with your first car?

2. How did you plan your first major road trip?

3. Which road trip moments became legendary stories?

Taking Risks

Life's greatest growth often lies just beyond our comfort zone. Each leap of faith, each bold choice, each adventure declined or accepted shapes our path forward.

1. What motivated you to step outside your comfort zone?

2. When did taking a big risk really pay off?

3. Which bold decisions shaped your future path?

Coming Home

Independence changes how we relate to our roots. How did your relationship with family evolve? Consider how your perspective on home and family shifted as you established your own life.

1. What changes did you notice when visiting your childhood home?

2. How did your relationship with family evolve during this time?

3. Which family traditions gained new meaning for you?

4

Meeting Mom

How did you and Mom find each other? We've always wondered about that magical moment when our family's love story first began.

First Encounter

Life can change in an instant when we meet someone special. What were the circumstances when you first met mom? Think about that encounter and the details that have stayed with you over the years.

1. What were you doing when you first crossed paths with mom?

2. When did you realize this meeting might be significant?

3. Which details from that first meeting stick in your memory?

Early Connection

The beginning of a relationship has its own rhythm. How did your relationship with mom begin to develop? Reflect on those first dates and interactions that laid the foundation for your future together.

1. What made you decide to ask mom out on that first date?

2. How did you plan those early dating experiences?

3. When did casual dating turn into something more regular?

Falling Deep

Some connections grow naturally into something profound. When did you realize your relationship with mom was becoming serious? Consider the experiences and moments that strengthened your connection.

1. What activities or interests brought you closer together?

2. How did you spend time getting to know each other better?

3. When did you start sharing future dreams with each other?

Meet the Parents

Family circles expand when hearts connect, bringing new dynamics, traditions, and relationships to navigate. These early meetings write the first chapters of family story.

1. What preparations did you make before meeting her family?

2. How did the first dinner with her parents actually unfold?

3. Which family member was the toughest to win over?

Perfect Proposal

Asking someone to share their life with you is both exciting and nerve-wracking. How did you decide to propose to mom? Reflect on the planning and details that went into this significant moment.

1. How did you know it was the right time to propose?

2. How did you manage to keep the surprise under wraps?

3. What elements went into planning the perfect proposal?

Wedding Plans

Planning a wedding involves countless decisions and compromises. What was your experience during the engagement period? Consider your involvement in the wedding plans.

1. What aspects of wedding planning did you take charge of?

2. When did the wedding preparations become most challenging?

3. Were there any funny or unexpected moments during the wedding planning process?

The Wedding Day

A wedding celebrates the beginning of a shared journey. What stands out from the day you got married? Think about the unexpected happenings that made your wedding day memorable.

1. What unexpected situations popped up during the wedding day?

2. How did the ceremony unfold compared to your plans?

3. Which wedding moments turned into favorite stories?

Honeymoon Tales

The first trip as a married couple creates special memories. Where did your new life together begin? Recall the destination, experiences, and meaningful moments from this celebration of your new status.

1. Where did you go for your honeymoon?

2. What was your favorite meal or food during the honeymoon?

3. Which experience became most memorable?

First Home

Establishing your first shared living space involves blending two lives. How did you build your first home together? Consider the practical and emotional aspects of creating a space that reflected both of you.

1. Where was your first home, and how did you decide on it?

2. What was the process of moving in like? Did anything funny or unexpected happen?

3. What did you do to make your first home feel comfortable and personal?

Growing Together

Early marriage is like learning to dance - sometimes stepping on toes, sometimes in perfect rhythm. Each day brings new lessons in the art of becoming truly partners in life.

1. What new things did you learn about each other after marriage?

2. How did you establish your daily routines as a couple?

3. When did you face your first major challenge together?

Building Future

New couples often dream about what their future might hold. What plans and hopes did you share in those early days? Reflect on the decisions that helped shape your path forward together.

1. What major goals did you set together early in marriage?

2. What was the first thing you saved money for as a couple?

3. How did you align your different visions for the future?

5

Becoming Dad

What was it like when you first became our father? We want to know how you felt holding us for the first time and how we changed your world forever.

The News

Finding out you're going to be a parent changes everything in an instant. What was your reaction when you learned a baby was on the way? Think about that life-changing moment and the emotions that came with this new reality.

1. What were you doing when you heard the news?

2. How did you start preparing for the baby?

3. When did you tell family and friends?

Birth Story

The arrival of a child is one of life's most profound moments. What was it like when your child was born? Recall the events, emotions, and first impressions from that remarkable day.

1. What happened on delivery day?

2. When did you first hold your child?

3. What moments from the birth stand out most in your memory?

Baby Milestones

Watching a child develop brings countless moments of wonder and pride. Which early milestones stand out in your memory? Consider those special "firsts" and how they affected you as a new parent.

1. What development changes surprised you?

2. How did you record special moments?

3. What baby milestones were the most exciting for you?

Growing Family

Each child brings new dynamics to family life. How did family grow and change over time? Reflect on the adjustments, challenges, and joys that came with each new family member.

1. How did you feel when you found out you were going to have another child?

2. What are some of your favorite memories of watching your children bond with each other?

3. What were some challenges you faced as your family grew?

Daily Parenting

Raising children involves countless everyday responsibilities. What did your regular routines as a dad look like? Think about the practical aspects of parenting and how you approached your daily role.

1. What daily tasks do you handle?

2. How do you organize childcare routines?

3. Which parenting tasks come naturally?

Learning Curve

No one becomes an expert parent overnight. What was your learning process like? Consider the challenges you faced, the mistakes that taught you lessons, and how you grew into your parenting role.

1. What parenting mistakes taught you most?

2. When did you start feeling confident?

3. Which skills took longest to master?

Changed Man

Becoming a parent often changes one's outlook and priorities. How did fatherhood change you? Reflect on the ways having children transformed your perspective, habits, and sense of self.

1. What habits changed after becoming a dad?

2. How did your priorities shift?

3. Which new skills developed naturally?

6

Growing Together

Can you share our family's special moments with us?
We treasure those everyday adventures, traditions, and
shared memories that have brought us closer together.

Daily Beginnings

Mornings set the tone for family life with their unique rhythms. How did you start each day? Think about the regular morning activities and how everyone worked together to begin the day.

1. What morning routine works best for the family?

2. When do you start the day's activities?

3. Which breakfast traditions does everyone enjoy?

Dinner Stories

Family dinners create space for sharing and connection. What happened around your dinner table? Think about the conversations that occurred during these daily gatherings.

1. What meals bring the family together?

2. How do you make dinner time special?

3. What dinner conversations do you remember most vividly?

Weekend Fun

Weekends write their own rules - time slows down, pajamas stay on longer, and ordinary moments stretch into extraordinary memories. These are the days when family time rules supreme.

1. What activities do you plan for weekends?

2. When do you schedule family outings?

3. Which weekend traditions last longest?

Holiday Magic

Holidays paint our family canvas with traditions passed down and new ones created. In these festive moments, ordinary days transform into treasured memories that mark our years together.

1. What holiday traditions do you maintain?

2. How do you prepare for celebrations?

3. Which holiday moments are most memorable?

Family Trip

Every family journey writes its own story – wrong turns become adventures, mishaps transform into memories, and shared discoveries bind us closer together on the road of life.

1. What makes a successful family vacation?

2. How do you handle travel challenges?

3. Which trip created the best stories?

Home Sweet Home

Within these walls, our daily life unfolds in countless small moments. Each room holds stories of laughter, tears, celebrations, and quiet togetherness that make a house our home.

1. What house rules work best?

2. How do you divide household tasks?

3. What areas of your home do you use the most?

Family Games

Games and recreational activities reveal family dynamics in special ways. What fun did family share together? Reflect on the competitive spirit, laughter, and bonding that came through playing together.

1. What games does everyone enjoy?

2. How do you make game nights special?

3. Which games create the most laughter?

Extended Family

Like branches of a great tree, extended family connects us to a wider world of love, tradition, and belonging. These gatherings write chapters in our family's continuing story.

1. What brings the extended family together?

2. How do you maintain family connections?

3. Which relatives do you see most often?

Special Days

Birthdays, achievements, and celebrations become the punctuation marks in family story. These special days remind us to pause, celebrate, and appreciate our journey together.

1. How do you mark family achievements?

2. When do you create special occasions?

3. Which birthday traditions continue yearly?

7

Career Journey

Dad, what has your work life been like? We're eager to hear about the jobs you've had and how you've used your talents throughout your career.

First Steps

Everyone starts somewhere in their professional life. What were your first working experiences? Think about those early jobs and how they introduced you to the world of work.

1. What was your first paid job?

2. How did you choose your initial career path?

3. When did you start your professional journey?

Career Path

Careers typically evolve over time through various positions and companies. How did your work life unfold? Consider the progression, changes, and growth in your professional journey.

1. What prompted your major career changes?

2. When did you find your professional direction?

3. What role had the biggest impact on shaping your career?

Tough Calls

Important crossroads appear throughout any career. What significant choices shaped your professional path? Reflect on the difficult decisions you encountered in your working life.

1. How do you handle workplace conflicts?

2. Was there a time you chose stability over taking a new opportunity?

3. Which professional challenge tested you most?

Skill Building

Professional growth requires continuous learning and adaptation. How did you develop your expertise? Think about the knowledge you gained throughout your working years.

1. What skills proved most valuable?

2. How do you stay current in your field?

3. What skill or certification was the most challenging for you to achieve?

Time Management

Effective professionals develop systems to manage their responsibilities. What strategies helped you stay organized and efficient? Think about the methods you used to handle your workload while making time for what matters.

1. What tools help you organize your day?

2. How do you handle multiple deadlines?

3. Which time-saving techniques work best?

Career Values

Personal principles guide how we approach our work. What values shaped your career decisions? Reflect on the standards, beliefs, and ideals that influenced your professional choices and behavior.

1. What professional standards guide your work?

2. How do you maintain work integrity?

3. Which values matter most in your field?

Work Wisdom

Experience provides valuable perspective on professional life. What wisdom did you gain from your working years? Think about the insights that came through your career experiences.

1. What advice would you give to new professionals?

2. How do you handle workplace pressure?

3. What career lesson was the hardest for you to learn?

8

Passion Projects

What activities make you happiest outside of work, Dad? We want to know about the hobbies and interests that have brought you joy and excitement over the years.

Leisure Pursuits

Everyone discovers activities that bring them joy outside of work and family. What hobbies have become important parts of your life? Think about the interests that have given you pleasure through the years.

1. What hobby has stayed with you the longest?

2. How do you carve out time for your personal interests?

3. Have your interests changed significantly over different periods of your life?

Creative Outlet

Creativity flows through different channels for each of us, finding its way through paint, words, music, or countless other forms. These expressions become the language of our inner world.

1. What creative projects have you completed?

2. How do you make time for your projects?

3. Which tools or materials do you use most?

Active Lifestyle

Physical activities contribute to both health and enjoyment. What sports have been part of your life? Reflect on the ways you've stayed active and the physical challenges you've embraced.

1. What sports or activities do you practice regularly?

2. How do you maintain your fitness routine?

3. What athletic accomplishments are you most proud of?

Collector's Corner

Gathering items of personal significance can become a meaningful pursuit. Have you collected anything special over the years? Think about the collections that have brought you joy.

1. What items do you collect and why?

2. How do you organize your collection?

3. Does any item in your collection have a particularly interesting story?

Mind Games

Mental stimulation comes in many forms, from games to lifelong learning. What activities engage your mind? Consider the puzzles, games, or intellectual pursuits that have challenged your thinking.

1. What mental challenges do you enjoy most?

2. How do you improve your problem-solving skills?

3. When do you make time for learning?

Workshop Stories

Creating or fixing things provides a special kind of satisfaction. What building or repair projects have you tackled? Reflect on your experiences working with tools and materials to make or fix things.

1. How did you learn your DIY skills?

2. When did you complete your first major project?

3. What project or creation are you most proud of?

Outdoor Enjoyment

In nature's embrace, we find both adventure and peace. Whether tending a garden or exploring wilderness, these moments connect us to something larger than ourselves.

1. What outdoor activities do you enjoy most?

2. How do you plan your nature adventures?

3. Which natural places do you visit regularly?

Favorite Reads

Books open doors to different worlds and perspectives. What role has reading played in your life? Consider the books that have been meaningful to you over the years.

1. What book first sparked your interest in reading?

2. How do you choose which books to read next?

3. Are there any books you've read over and over again?

Movie Memories

Movies offer entertainment while also marking different chapters in our lives. What films have been meaningful to you over the years? Think about the stories and characters that have left a lasting impression.

1. What movies do you remember watching over and over?

2. How did you discover your favorite genres or directors?

3. How did you pick movies for family movie nights?

Digital World

The digital world has transformed how we pursue interests and connect with others. How have you interacted with technology as a hobby? Consider your experiences with digital tools and tech-related projects.

1. What technology projects interest you?

2. How do you keep up with digital trends?

3. Are there any online communities you're an active part of?

Shared Interests

Some passions grow stronger when shared with others. What interests have you pursued alongside friends or groups? Reflect on how shared passions have connected you with others.

1. What group activities do you participate in?

2. How do you connect with others through hobbies?

3. When do you organize group activities?

9

Wisdom & Dreams

What life lessons do you want to share with us, Dad?
We're curious about both your hopes for our future
and the important wisdom you've gathered along your
journey.

Life Compass

Some principles stand eternal, like lighthouse beacons guiding ships through storms. These core values become the foundation upon which all worthy futures are built.

1. What are the three most important rules you live by?

2. How do you make difficult decisions when facing two good options?

3. What daily habits help you stay aligned with your values?

Success Recipe

True success has many ingredients, mixed in proportions unique to each life. Yet some essential elements remain constant, creating the foundation for a life well-lived.

1. What practical steps led to your biggest achievements?

2. How do you balance different aspects of life successfully?

3. When did you realize what success meant to you?

Inner Strength

Character, like a mighty oak, grows stronger through life's storms. These inner resources become our foundation when external supports waver.

1. What daily practices help build mental toughness?

2. How do you maintain focus during difficult times?

3. Which challenges have taught you the most valuable lessons?

Trust Tests

Trust, like fine crystal, takes time to build but shatters in an instant. Through experiences of loyalty and betrayal, we learn the delicate art of placing faith in others.

1. What signs help you evaluate someone's trustworthiness?

2. How do you verify people's reliability in business?

3. When did you learn to set boundaries with others?

Hard Choices

Life's crossroads rarely come with clear signposts. Through difficult decisions, we learn to navigate the complex terrain between right and right, between good and better.

1. What method do you use to make difficult decisions?

2. How do you weigh short-term versus long-term benefits?

3. Which tough decision proved most beneficial later?

Future Dreams

Like stars guiding sailors across vast oceans, our dreams for those we love light the way forward. These hopes we carry become the constellations by which our family charts its course.

1. What specific goals do you have for our family in the next 5-10 years?

2. How do you plan to help each family member achieve their dreams?

3. Which practical steps are you taking today to build our family's future?

More Stories to Collect

Every parent and grandparent carries a treasure trove of memories waiting to be shared. Our beautifully crafted keepsake books help capture these precious stories before they fade with time.

Our Family Story Series

Dad Story   **Mom Story**   **Grandpa Story**   **Grandma Story**

Available at:

- Amazon

- Barnes & Noble

- Major online bookstores

Give a gift that grows more precious with time - because every family member's story deserves to be told, shared, and treasured.

www.ingramcontent.com/pod-product-compliance
Lightning Source LLC
Chambersburg PA
CBHW051328120626
46547CB00015B/2441